Cornerstones of Freedom

The Battle of the Little Bighorn

R. Conrad Stein

CHILDREN'S PRESS®
A Division of Grolier Publishing
New York • London • Hong Kong • Sydney
Danbury, Connecticut

Library of Congress Cataloging-in-Publication Data

Stein, R. Conrad.
The Battle of the Little Bighorn / R. Conrad Stein.
    p. cm.—(Cornerstones of freedom)
    Includes index.
    Summary: The story of the worst defeat ever suffered by the
United States Army at the hands of the American Indians near the
Little Bighorn River in Montana on June 25, 1876.
    ISBN 0-516-20296-0 (lib.bdg.)   0-516-26136-3 (pbk.)
    1. Little Bighorn, Battle of the, Mont., 1876—Juvenile literature.
2. Custer, George Armstrong, 1839–1876—Juvenile literature.
[1. Little Bighorn, Battle of the, Mont., 1876. 2. Custer, George
Armstrong, 1839–1876.] I. Title. II. Series.
E83.876.S727 1997
973.8`2—dc20
                                                                  96-28191
                                                                      CIP
                                                                       AC

In the summer of 1876, the United States celebrated its one hundredth birthday. Throughout the thirty-eight states, church bells pealed and fireworks exploded in the night. Americans rejoiced in the freedom and democracy that had been established one century before.

The American Indians who lived on the Great Plains, however, did not share the joy that the rest of the country felt. The Great Plains spread between the Mississippi River and the Rocky Mountains. For hundreds of years, most of the Plains Indians had lived in tipi villages and hunted buffalo on this vast grassland. But the Plains people were unable to stop the United States's expansion from the East. By the early 1870s, many American Indians of the northern Great Plains had signed treaties that forced them to live on reservations set up by the United States government.

The Plains Indians hunted buffalo and lived in tipis.

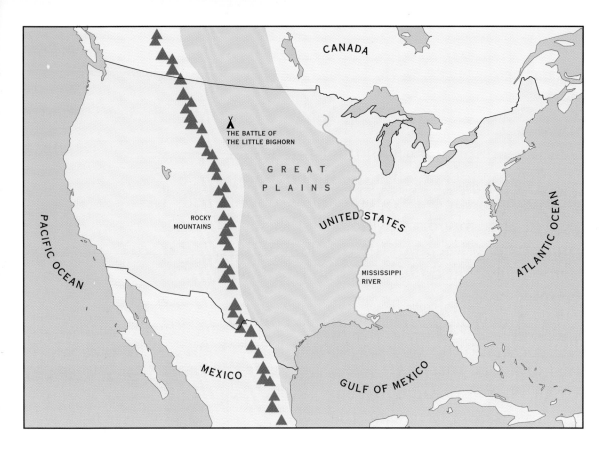

CANADA

THE BATTLE OF
THE LITTLE BIGHORN

G R E A T
P L A I N S

ROCKY
MOUNTAINS

UNITED STATES

MISSISSIPPI
RIVER

PACIFIC OCEAN

ATLANTIC OCEAN

MEXICO

GULF OF MEXICO

The land between the Mississippi River and the Rocky Mountains was called the Great Plains.

One large reservation in present-day South Dakota sat at the edge of the Black Hills. This region of forests and spectacular granite crags was considered sacred land. The Lakota people of the Plains believed that the Black Hills were the final resting grounds of their ancestors. A government treaty signed in 1868 guaranteed this sacred land would belong to the Lakota American Indians forever. Not long after, however, traces of gold were discovered in the Black Hills region. By 1875, more than a thousand miners and prospectors had entered the Black Hills illegally to search for gold. Rather than evict the miners from American-

Indian land, the U.S. government sent troops to protect the miners. A fierce argument over the ownership of the Black Hills began. Eventually, war on the Great Plains looked inevitable.

Prospectors and miners arrived in the Black Hills to search for gold (left). The Black Hills region of South Dakota (below) was sacred land to the Lakota people.

The largest and most powerful American-Indian nation in the northern Great Plains was the Lakota. Even before the struggle over the Black Hills, many Lakota bands had already refused to leave their lands and move onto the government reservations. One of these groups was led by a medicine man named Sitting Bull. He was a shaman, a person with the ability to heal sickness, to communicate with animals, and to foretell the future. Sitting Bull once said that when he walked barefoot over the grasses of the Plains, he could "hear the very heartbeat of the holy Earth."

Before dawn one early summer day in 1876, Sitting Bull sensed that war between his people and the United States government was certain. He wanted to prepare the Lakota for the difficulties that were ahead. Sitting Bull donned a scarlet-colored blanket and sat with his back against a sacred tree. Facing east, toward the rising sun, he recited prayers and performed an ancient ritual called the Sun Dance. The ritual was designed to help Sitting Bull see into the spirit world.

Part of the ritual required that Sitting Bull deny himself food and water for twenty-four hours. During that time, he had a vision from the spirit world. In the vision, he saw white soldiers and their horses falling down in a Lakota camp. Finally, Sitting Bull collapsed.

When he awoke, he told his people of his spirit-world vision. They all believed it could mean only that a great Lakota victory lay ahead in the coming war with the United States Army.

Sitting Bull was the Lakota chief whose spirit-world vision convinced him that a great Indian victory against the U.S. Army was about to occur.

General George Crook

In preparation for war on the northern Great Plains, the United States government had commanded that all American Indians who had not already moved onto reservations do so immediately. Those who refused were declared "hostiles." U.S. Army soldiers were sent to the region with orders to force all hostile Indians onto reservation land.

In early June 1876, cavalry under the command of General George Crook rode along Rosebud Creek in present-day Montana. General

American Indians were forced from their land and moved to reservations established by the U.S. government.

Crook was an experienced Indian fighter who followed a simple practice: always employ American-Indian scouts and warriors when waging war with other Indians. Riding with Crook's 1,300 cavalry troops were 260 Shoshone and Crow scouts. Both tribes were enemies of the Lakota. On the morning of June 17, Crook shouted the command for his long column of soldiers to halt. He allowed them to rest while the horses grazed along the creek bank. Once the march stopped, the Shoshone and Crow scouts became uneasy. They knew that by not moving, they became easy targets for angry Lakota Indians. All knew that the feared Lakota leader, Crazy Horse, lurked somewhere in the region. Crazy Horse was famous for leading surprise attacks.

Suddenly a Shoshone scout on horseback thundered into the soldiers' ranks. "Lakota!" he shouted. "Many Lakota!" Shots rang out in the distance. Officers shouted orders, and soldiers scrambled to saddle their horses. General Crook looked toward the horizon. There he saw hundreds of Lakota and Cheyenne on horseback, galloping toward his unprepared troops. Many of the Indians were armed with rifles, others carried bows and arrows. With guns firing, Crook's Crow and Shoshone scouts rushed to meet the charge. These American-Indian allies saved Crook's command by fighting off the Lakota and Cheyenne, and giving Crook's cavalrymen time to take up arms.

The battle took place along 3 miles (5 kilometers) of Rosebud Creek. The normally quiet creek valley exploded with sounds—horses neighing, Indians shouting war cries, and rifles firing. General Crook tried to counter the Indians'

General Crook and his army were defeated by the Lakota at Rosebud Creek.

The Little Bighorn River

attack by sending a large unit of cavalry toward the enemy's rear. But the attempt failed. The Indians concentrated their attacks on the newly weakened point in Crook's line.

Finally, Crook's men forced the Lakota to break off their attack and withdraw. Crook later claimed victory in the Battle of the Rosebud. But the battle was hardly a triumph for the U.S. Army. Ten of Crook's men were killed, and about thirty were seriously wounded. After the battle, the general tended to the wounded, replenished his supplies, and temporarily called off the search for Indians. By then, the Indian scouts and the army officers were sure that the gifted warrior, Crazy Horse, was commanding the Lakota warriors. Crook was worried because he believed that Crazy Horse had survived the battle. The general was certain that Crazy Horse would lead the Lakota in another attack. Eight days later, the Lakota and the army clashed once more, this time about 30 miles (48 km) to the north, along a river called the Little Bighorn.

George Armstrong Custer graduated from West Point in 1861.

Joining Crook on the Great Plains was the 7th Cavalry Regiment, commanded by a 36-year-old lieutenant colonel named George Armstrong Custer. In 1861, Custer graduated from the United States Military Academy at West Point with the lowest grades in his class. But during the American Civil War (1861–1865), he distinguished himself as one of the most successful cavalry officers in the Union army. Fearless in combat, he led his men on blistering attacks against the Confederate army.

When the Civil War ended in 1865, Custer was transferred to the Western frontier. To the American public, he became a hero for his battles against American Indians. Trim, athletic, and standing 6 feet (183 centimeters) tall, Custer was a dashing cavalry leader. During the Civil War he designed his own uniforms, which featured black velveteen decorations laced with gold braids. His trademark was his shoulder-length blond hair. American Indians called him Long Hair. His soldiers nicknamed him Iron Butt, because of his ability to ride his horse for days, seemingly without fatigue.

Throughout the army, officers talked about what they called the "Custer luck." All agreed that Custer was a brave officer who always seemed to be in the right place at the right time. His talents attracted the attention of his superior officers, and he was often the subject of newspaper articles. It was rumored that Custer might someday run for political office, perhaps even the presidency.

George Armstrong Custer became a successful cavalry officer during the American Civil War (1861–1865).

As Custer led his six hundred soldiers into the hostile territory surrounding the Little Bighorn River, he had no idea of the fate that awaited him. In the days following the Rosebud battle, more Lakota had arrived at the Little Bighorn to join Crazy Horse and Sitting Bull. Bands of Cheyenne and Arapaho had also gathered in the Montana hunting grounds. All of the Indians were frustrated by reservation life. They were also outraged by U.S. government claims on their sacred Black Hills. But the Indians were encouraged by the victory at Rosebud Creek. Night after night, the Indians held victory dances to celebrate Crazy Horse's triumph over General Crook. But Sitting Bull did not participate in the celebrations. He believed that the Rosebud battle fell short of the victory he had visualized during his Sun Dance. In that vision, hundreds of soldiers fell to their deaths inside an Indian camp. To Sitting Bull, that spirit-world dream had not yet been fulfilled.

On June 25, 1876, Custer's scouts looked down from their camp at a stunning sight—thousands of tipis stood on the western side of the twisting Little Bighorn River. Later reports estimated that 7,000 Indians, including at least 1,500 warriors, were camped on the riverbank. It was one of the largest gatherings of Plains Indians in history.

Cheyenne and Lakota tipis along the Little Bighorn River—June 25, 1876

Scouts reported the huge camp to Lieutenant Colonel Custer. The commander pondered his next step. Custer felt confident that he could order a surprise attack on the Indians in the camp. He knew that there was no record of Plains Indians ever confronting an entire regiment of United States cavalry and defeating them. Custer may also have been concerned that the Indians would escape and avoid removal to the government reservations.

Following the reports of his American-Indian scouts, Custer planned an attack on the Indians.

Major Marcus Reno

Reno and his cavalrymen charged into the southern end of the Indian camp.

Custer decided to divide his regiment into three units and order a full-scale attack on the Indians. In the first wave of the attack, commanded by Major Marcus Reno, 140 cavalrymen charged into the southern end of the Indian camp. From the beginning, the attack faltered as Reno's charge was stopped by Lakota and Cheyenne warriors. A Cheyenne named Two Moon later reported, "The air was full of smoke and dust. I saw the soldiers fall back and drop into the riverbed like buffalo fleeing."

Frantically, Reno's soldiers took up defensive positions above the river. After about thirty minutes of bitter fighting, they were joined by

units commanded by Captain Frederick Benteen. Benteen was supposed to lead the second force in Custer's assault. Instead, Reno, Benteen, and their men desperately defended against the attacking American Indians. Both officers sensed that the battle had taken a disastrous turn. They were cavalrymen who were trained to charge at the enemy, not to fight in hand-to-hand combat. Reno ordered a retreat, which resulted in the loss of about one-third of the men in his command. Benteen also ordered his men to retreat.

This is the site above the river where Reno's unit was joined by Captain Frederick Benteen and his men.

Unaware of Reno and Benteen's retreat, Custer circled to the northern end of the camp to strike a third attack on the enemy. By dividing his regiment into several groups, Custer followed a strategy that had been successful for him in the Civil War, and in previous clashes with American-Indian warriors. Attacking an enemy from different sides was an aggressive tactic, one designed to spread confusion and fear in the ranks of the enemy. Against this huge Indian army, however, the attack succeeded only in leaving Custer's divided units hopelessly outnumbered.

During Civil War battles, Custer learned that dividing a unit into several groups before attacking an enemy was usually successful.

Reports indicate that a force of between one thousand and two thousand warriors led by Crazy Horse was racing to meet Custer in battle. Unlike the soldiers of the U.S. Army, these men did not belong to formal units. Traditionally, American-Indian warriors followed leaders who had proven to be brave and resourceful in the past. Crazy Horse was already a legend on the Great Plains. His battle cry was simple and direct, "It is a good day to fight; it is a good day to die." All warriors heeded his call.

Custer and his cavalrymen were no match for the American Indians.

This depiction of fallen Lakota warriors was drawn by a Lakota Indian. It reflects the importance of the battle to the American Indians, who saw it as a great victory over white expansion into their sacred lands.

Suddenly Custer's line of cavalrymen was attacked from both sides by shouting Lakota and Cheyenne warriors. A thirteen-year-old Lakota boy named Black Elk watched from a distance. "On a hill there was a big dust," Black Elk later recalled. "And our warriors were whirling in and out of the dust just like swallows, and many guns were going off. The women were singing to cheer the men fighting across the river in the dust on the hill." Another observer was the Lakota medicine man, Sitting Bull. He, too, was unable to see the fighting clearly because of the cloud of sand and smoke that covered the area. But Sitting Bull believed that this was the battle he saw in the Sun Dance ritual vision. He knew then that the Lakota and Cheyenne would defeat the U.S. soldiers.

Surrounded by about two thousand Indians, Custer's troops had to dismount from their horses. They tried to fight one-on-one with the Indians, but the troops could not fire their guns and hold on to their panicked horses at the same time. A Lakota warrior named Low Dog later reported, "As we rushed upon them, the white soldiers dismounted to fire, but they did poor shooting. They held their horses' reins on one arm while they were shooting, but their horses were so frightened that they pulled the men all around, and a great many of their shots went up in the air and did us no harm."

According to many Indian reports, Custer's men fought with great courage. In the blinding dust, they used their rifles as clubs to strike out at the warriors. Sitting Bull later said, "I tell no lies about dead men. These men who came with the Long Hair (Custer) were as good men as ever fought." Years later the Lakota warrior White Bull told of a violent hand-to-hand struggle with a single soldier. Some historians believe that soldier was George Armstrong Custer. White Bull said, "I charged in. A tall, well-built soldier with yellow hair and mustache saw me coming. . . . He threw his rifle at me without shooting. I dodged it. We grabbed each other and wrestled there in the dust and smoke. It was like fighting in a fog. This soldier was very strong and brave. . . . Finally I broke free. He drew his pistol. I wrenched it out of his hand and struck him three or four times on the head, knocked him over, shot him in the head, and then fired at his heart."

White Bull, who may have been the Lakota who killed Custer

Outnumbered almost five to one, the army soldiers had no chance. The Battle of the Little Bighorn lasted about an hour. Custer and all 210 soldiers under his immediate command were killed. The only survivors were one horse and a Crow scout named Curley. Reno, Benteen, and about 300 soldiers survived the battle. About 1,000 American-Indian warriors also survived. The defeat of the 7th Cavalry Regiment was the worst ever suffered by the U.S. Army at the hands of American Indians.

The only two survivors of Custer's command were an American-Indian scout named Curley (above) and a horse named Comanche (right).

News of Custer's fate reached the rest of the United States around July 4, 1876. A long-awaited Fourth of July celebration in Philadelphia, Pennsylvania, was supposed to be the highlight of the banner centennial year. But the jubilant mood of the confident young nation was shattered by news of the events along the Little Bighorn River. Americans were shocked to hear that a skilled regiment of its army had been defeated by the Plains Indians.

Today, white markers on the Little Bighorn Battlefield show where soldiers' bodies were found.

Artists depicted Custer (standing, center) fighting bravely in what became known as Custer's Last Stand (below). Newspapers throughout the country carried stories of the battle (below, right).

In the days and weeks that followed, writers and artists rendered the battle in glorious terms. Newspaper reporters hailed Custer as a hero. In hundreds of drawings and paintings, artists pictured Custer bravely fighting to the death against the Indian warriors. Eventually, the Battle of the Little Bighorn came to be called Custer's Last Stand.

The battle, however, proved to be the Plains Indians' last stand.

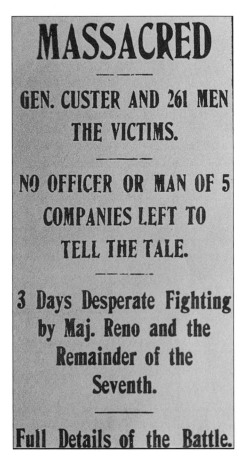

MASSACRED

GEN. CUSTER AND 261 MEN THE VICTIMS.

NO OFFICER OR MAN OF 5 COMPANIES LEFT TO TELL THE TALE.

---

3 Days Desperate Fighting by Maj. Reno and the Remainder of the Seventh.

Full Details of the Battle.

Embarrassed by the defeat, the U.S. Army sent one-third of its total forces to the northern Great Plains. Seeking revenge, the soldiers stormed into Indian villages, often burning them to the ground. By the spring of 1877, almost all of the Plains people had been forced onto reservations. Government agents decreased the size of the reservations in order to create more room for white settlers from the East. The Black Hills became the property of the United States government.

U.S. Army soldiers burned Indian villages to avenge the defeat at Little Bighorn.

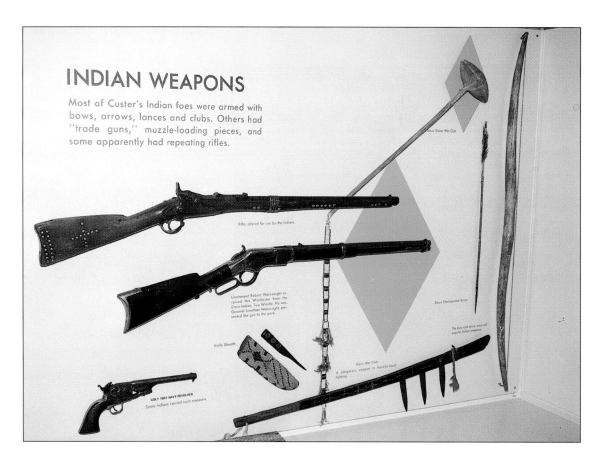

INDIAN WEAPONS

Most of Custer's Indian foes were armed with bows, arrows, lances and clubs. Others had "trade guns," muzzle-loading pieces, and some apparently had repeating rifles.

Sioux Stone War Club

Rifle, altered for use by the Indians.

Lieutenant Robert Wainwright received this Winchester from the Crow Indian, Two Whistle. His son, General Jonathan Wainwright, presented the gun to the park.

Sioux Steel-pointed Arrow

Knife Sheath

The bow and arrow were still popular Indian weapons.

Sioux War Club
A dangerous weapon in hand-to-hand fighting

COLT 1861 NAVY REVOLVER
Some Indians carried such weapons.

Indian weapons (above) and recently discovered soldiers' relics (right) are on display in the museum at the Little Bighorn Battlefield National Monument.

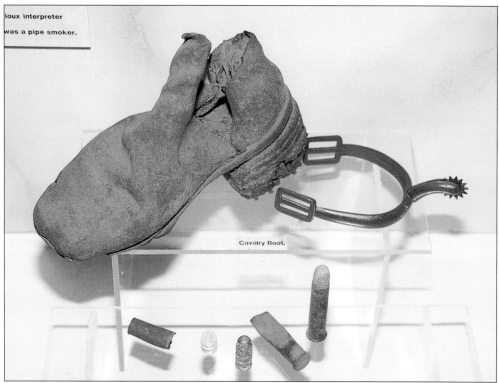

ioux interpreter
was a pipe smoker.

Cavalry Boot.

Today, the battlefield site in Montana, called the Little Bighorn Battlefield National Monument, is visited by thousands of people each year. The battlefield is equally significant to whites and American Indians. To whites, Little Bighorn is the site of a tragic massacre of soldiers killed in the line of duty. American Indians, however, consider the battle to be the only time the Indians successfully defended their homeland against white settlement. Almost everyone agrees that the battle site is sacred because so many lives were lost there.

Monuments pay tribute to the soldiers and Indians who died at the Battle of the Little Bighorn.

GLOSSARY

band – group of people

cavalry – army unit whose soldiers ride on horses

cavalrymen – soldiers in an army unit who ride on horseback

centennial – celebration marking a 100th birthday

column – long row of soldiers

frontier

crag – steep rock or cliff

fatigue – weariness or exhaustion

foe – enemy

foretell – to know about a future event before it happens

frontier – the farthermost area of a settled or developed territory

regiment – military unit

ritual – ceremony performed according to religious law or social custom

tipi

sacred – place or object considered to be very holy and worthy of respect

tipi – cone-shaped dwelling used by American Indians of the Plains

trademark – distinguishing characteristic

velveteen – type of cloth that is similar to velvet

TIMELINE

Sitting Bull born **1831**

1839 George Armstrong Custer born

Crazy Horse born **1849**

1861 Custer graduates from West Point;
Civil War begins

1865 Civil War ends; Custer transferred to
western frontier

1868 Black Hills allotted to Lakota

Gold discovered in Black Hills **1874**

Gold miners invade Black Hills **1875**

1876

Lakota defeated by U.S. Army; Black Hills **1877**
become property of federal government;
Crazy Horse dies

March: General
Crook arrives

June 17: Crook's
army attacked
by Lakota at
Rosebud Creek

Sitting Bull dies **1890**

June 25: Battle of
the Little Bighorn

July 4: News
of Custer's defeat
dampens
Centennial
celebrations

INDEX *(**Boldface** page numbers indicate illustrations.)*

PHOTO CREDITS

©: Archive Photos: 15 bottom, 22; Corbis-Bettmann: 1, 5 top, 7, 16 top, 19, 31 bottom right, 31 left; Denver Public Library, Western History Department: 8 top, 10, 15 top, 23; James P. Rowan: cover; North Wind Picture Archives: 3, 8 bottom, 24, 25, 27, 30 bottom; Reinhard Brucker: 2, 5 bottom, 11, 17, 26 right, 28, 29, 30 top; Stock Montage, Inc.: 20, 26 left; U.S. Army Military History Institute: 9, 16 bottom, 18; U.S. Military Academy: 12, 31 top right; UPI/Corbis-Bettmann: 13.

Map by TJS Design

ABOUT THE AUTHOR

R. Conrad Stein was born in Chicago, Illinois. After serving in the Marine Corps he attended the University of Illinois, where he received a degree in history. He later studied in Mexico, where he received an advanced degree. A full-time writer, Mr. Stein has published more than eighty books for young readers. He lives in Chicago with his wife and their daughter, Janna.